Anonymous

The Duty of Citizens in the present Crisis

Second Edition

Anonymous

The Duty of Citizens in the present Crisis
Second Edition

ISBN/EAN: 9783337139537

Printed in Europe, USA, Canada, Australia, Japan

Cover: Foto ©ninafisch / pixelio.de

More available books at **www.hansebooks.com**

THE
DUTY OF CITIZENS
IN THE
PRESENT CRISIS.

THE SECOND EDITION.

The real Enemies of a free State, are such of its own Citizens as undermine its Liberties.

LONDON:

PRINTED FOR R. H. WESTLEY, NO. 201, OPPOSITE ST. CLEMENT'S CHURCH, STRAND.

1793.

ADVERTISEMENT.

THE Address which forms the first pages of this work, was written for one of the late popular meetings. As many Gentlemen who then desired to become subscribing parties, have since requested copies, it is now presented to them with elucidations.

THE

DUTY OF CITIZENS, &c.

SECTION I.

ADDRESS TO THE PEOPLE OF ENGLAND.

WE who now addrefs ourfelves,—to the People of England,—as an argument for a juft claim to attention, begin by declaring, that we are not men enlifted under any political banner, or poffeffed of either place, penfion, or emolument from Government; confequently, we cannot be actuated by motives of private intereft, or political influence; but pride ourfelves on having a nobler ftake depending than either politics or patronage can beftow,—our unalienable Rights as Englifhmen; fecurity of Perfon and Property—Liberty—our Kindred, and our Country!

These it is our duty to protect against lawless invaders. Such a stake is indeed sacred! and although it be ours only in common with every individual, yet our being the Fathers of numerous Families, by giving us a manifold and important risque in the serenity and prosperity of the State, invests us with the more indisputable right to exert our utmost abilities, and to invite all reasonable persons to join with us, in conducing to the peace and good order of the Kingdom; and in supporting, with united efforts, its present Constitution of King, Lords, and Commons, thoroughly convinced, as we are, from the experience of ages, and the survey of surrounding States, that no other Constitution, of whatever denomination, found in the page of history, has been more effectually calculated to afford the same Blessings of Liberty, Security, and Protection! Perfection is not the lot of human nature, but as near it as human institutions

can

can, the well digested Theory of our Constitution has approached: a Constitution, which Britons have contemplated, with an honest pride, as the just object of their own glory, and the envy of the European world!

This Fabric of Liberty,—this Monument of our Security, we well know to have been the progressive work of ages, effected by men of profound wisdom, and unsullied integrity. These Statesmen, so able, and distinguished, did also adopt every wise precaution to furnish individuals, in cases of wrong, with the means of redress: And, therefore, as political defects arise, or abuses are introduced, by the excellence of a Constitution, formed of three equal Estates, relief may be always at hand. These three Estates, of *distinct* interest, and of *equal* power, were deliberately formed to act on a System established on the jealous principle

ciple of "Check upon Check," that in all cafes of encroachment, error, or abufe, each might correct the other; and preferve the well balanced order of the State. And, by which means, we poffefs the valuable Right of always controuling the PRACTICE of this our beautiful THEORY;—a Right, which, in all emergencies, has been happily exercifed, and can be effectually reforted to;—a Right, from which we ever have, and muft always find relief; equally well adapted to repel injury, and to court the improvements of wifdom and experience. And, here, let us remind our Countrymen, (of what nothing but a miftaken infatuation can ever caufe them to lofe fight) that, out of three, the People already poffefs *one equal part of the national Sovereignty*; confequently, are in themfelves, through the medium of their Reprefentatives, the Houfe of Commons, one perfect branch of the Government, equal in power, dignity,

dignity, and influence, with each of the other two eftates feparately taken, and entitled, on all occafions, even to put a negative on the proceedings of either or both.

By thefe wife precautions are our Liberties, Lives, and Property, fecured from the invafion of tyranny or defpotifm :—bleffings that are not enjoyed under any other form of Government! Let not, therefore any clafs of Britons fuffer themfelves to be deceived into an opinion, that they are defpifed as Cyphers in the STATE, it being the PEOPLE only whom the Legiflature can acknowledge in the perfons of their Reprefentatives—the WHOLE HOUSE OF COMMONS, from amongft whom, even the MINISTERS of the COUNTRY, are generally appointed for the exprefs duty of guarding and preferving their Rights and Privileges:—and fo long as this important branch of the Legiflature—the Houfe of Commons, fhall preferve its own Dignity, and Independence, by faithfully adhering to the true principle and fpirit of its inftitution, it is morally impoffible, even admitting that at intervals they may be fubject to fome partial invafion, that the RIGHTS of the PEOPLE can ever be annihilated.

Such is the admirable Conftitution bequeathed to us by our anceftors, under the moft facred injunctions to preferve it:— and as human efforts were infufficient to fecure it from the ravages of time, and the encroachment of error, and abufe, they wifely and exprefsly provided the People with the power of correcting them, through the medium of the Houfe of Commons, who are not only perfectly competent, but muft feel it to be their firft duty, and trueft intereft, to preferve the facred and effential balance of the State.

Let

Let us now advert to some of the strong Pillars of our protection,—the Safeguards of our Freedom. We have Magna Charta for the Basis of our Liberty. The Habeas Corpus Act to preserve us from unjust imprisonment. A Grand Jury, formed from among OURSELVES, to secure us from unfair, or unnecessary prosecutions. And petty Juries, formed also from among OURSELVES, to protect us against unjust punishment in Criminal Cases, and against wanton deprivation of property in Civil. If dissatisfied with the decisions of these Juries so chosen, we have the means of appealing to other tribunals equally well calculated for Relief against oppression, and even against error: and, last of all, we have the benefit of applying to the Benignity of a Throne which we OURSELVES have constituted, for that mercy that inexorable Justice could never grant: yet, this mercy,—this power of pardoning—this last Refuge of unhappy Criminals,

nals, is the only judicial inequality or superiority which the monarch possesses over either of the other two Estates.

Let not, therefore, any jealousy or tenaciousness of power, (feelings but too natural to human nature,) delude the good sense of Englishmen to deceitful Phantoms artfully placed between us and the solid blessings in our possession! The power of the monarchical branch of the Legislature over the other two, and that wisely created by OURSELVES is no more than the Power of HUMANITY, of BENEVOLENCE, and of REWARD—the Power of doing GOOD!— Whence then any apprehension of Injury?— Yet, great pains have been taken, and alarm industriously propagated to set the King and the People at variance with each other! And the example of a neighbouring Nation has been held out to us for this very purpose. We presume neither to question, or to condemn,

demn, where we cannot possibly have a right to judge. As Citizens of the world, we wish Peace and Prosperity to France, and to all Nations! But, one great truth must be obvious to ALL; and that is, *the utter impossibility of the example of France being ever fitted to England.* The French did not, like ourselves, possess the blessings of Freedom: the Yoke of despotic Laws, the interpretation of which was committed to Judges who corruptly purchased their places by public auction, had galled them to DESPERATION; and they have the inexhaustible Resource of an immense Territory, which may *possibly* prove competent to the Support of their whole Nation; and on their own principles. Whereas ours, is so limited and circumscribed, as to dictate the *absolute* Necessity of resorting to NAVIGATION, COMMERCE, ARTS, and MANUFACTURES for SUPPORT!—It is then manifest, that were these our necessary resources neglected, or destroyed ed by convulsion, tumult, or any other cause, we must be driven to the savage, naked condition of our ancestors: and ranging the forest for food, must substitute *Paint* for *Cloathing* ; and become a helpless prey to the first foreign tyrant who might chuse to invade our little Island, and fix our doom!—Ye, therefore, who are Fathers, or mean to be so, sacrifice not your rising generation, nor endanger the peace and future happiness of our much envied nation under its present provident and protecting Constitution, to any temporary delusion, or visionary schemes of restless individuals, whom jealousy, passion, or envy, render blind to the social benefits which they attempt to interrupt!

We learn with grief, the present anxiety and alarm. We trust that they are not only premature, but will appear to be wholly without cause. However they may have been diffused, when we find the peace of
Society

Society disturbed, and domestic security threatened, it becomes the duty of all good citizens to unite in exertions to preserve them: and to endeavour, by an union of minds and interests, to form a strong and protecting shield against growing Virulence and eventful Convulsion. We, therefore, most solemnly invite, All the REASONABLE and WELL-DISPOSED PEOPLE OF ENGLAND, to join in support of the KING AND CONSTITUTION, as settled at the Revolution. In this case, we know no distinction of Party: for, however Parties may differ on subordinate points, we are confident there cannot be a difference on these fundamental Principles.

Our liberal-minded Countrymen will not suppose, that we have any other inducement to make this invitation to " UNION AND GOOD ORDER," than that of having

ing a similar Interest in the State with themselves: but, they will remember, that it is the call of Britons, proud and tenacious of their Liberties—jealous of their Birthrights—affectionate to their Kinsmen—and hospitable to all mankind! That it is a call to incite them to preserve those resources, which have produced so many inestimable Blessings,—so much real Liberty and true happiness to Britons,—and have made them the admiration and envy of the whole world: that it is, in fact, the Call of THEMSELVES:—the Call of their KING and COUNTRY:—that it is the Call of their CHILDREN, and all who look up to them for PROTECTION;—of every pledge they hold most sacred!—It is indeed a Call so sacred, that were our Ancestors to arise from the Grave, it would be to set the example of OBEDIENCE, and to reproach those who should fail in that indespensable duty. Surely it must have been their last awful

awful injunction, to preserve this holy Bequest of liberty perfect and unsullied to the latest posterity! These are the principles on which we apply to your feelings as Britons, and to your allegiance as Citizens and Subjects.

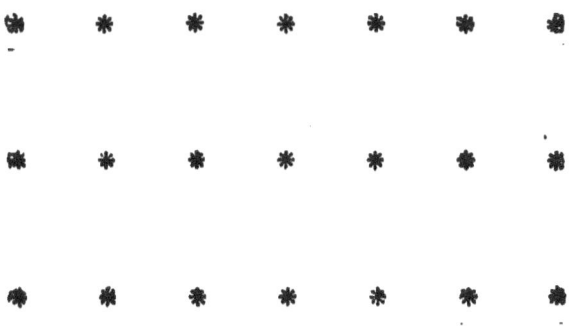

SECTION

SECTION II.

OF THE GENERAL SUBJECT.

THE foregoing Addrefs was intended for the Prefs previous to the meeting of Parliament, when the public mind laboured under much dark agitation, and every individual was tempted to regard his neighbour as a traitor to his Country, and an enemy to the good order of fociety. That alarm has now fubfided, and appears to be followed by a general amazement, that the caufe fhould fo fuddenly have vanifhed: but, every true friend to the Conftitution muft rejoice to obferve, that it has demonftrated—what never ought to have been ferioufly doubted, that neither contrivance nor plot can fhake the loyalty of Britons; that their fpirits once rouzed and united, they dread not a combination of the whole world; that to difturb the welfare of thefe united Kingdoms, is, internally, as difficult

cult, as externally, the attempt would be formidable and hazardous! that Great Britain is inhabited by good Citizens, whofe character for moderation, firmnefs, and good fellowfhip, are not to be diverted from the true interefts of the State, of which they are the real fupport; that their loyalty and attachment to the Houfe of Hanover bid defiance to fufpicion; and that his Majefty reigns in the affections of the people, notwithftanding the pains which have induftrioufly been taken to fet them both at variance.

Such is the conftruction of the late rumoured infurrections of the people!—Such is the tower of ftrength on which his Majefty can always fafely rely in the hour of doubt, difficulty, and danger! Such too are the true features and delineations of the faithful Citizens of thefe united Kingdoms; and on which I have the happinefs to
congratulate

congratulate my country!—Fidelity thus tramples on fuspicion, and real attachment instantly extinguishes imaginary disaffection!

Thus we stigmatize all such slanderous imputations, and expose the dark designs of hypocrisy and corruption, and openly declare to the world, " that the PEOPLE, can never have an interest in disorder."

With sorrow, I afterwards learnt, that under a false impression, and as if this declared sense of the people were still doubted, one of our Representatives in Parliament, had signified an intention of moving for a partial suspension of the *Habeas Corpus* Act, an intention justly reprobated by that firm admirer and supporter of our Constitution; that vigilant and incorrupt Statesmen, the " FRIEND OF THE PEOPLE," whose pride is to merit their esteem, and whose

life

life has been devoted to the defence of their Liberties.

The bare suggestion of such measures, and the general state of the Empire, induces me to obtrude on my Fellow Citizens, a few admonitions respecting the duties the Common--weal impose, and which, in my opinion, the society, in which we live has a right to require at the hands of each of us, being all equally interested to maintain and preserve the blessings we derive from it: duties, which it is not merely necessary to acknowledge; we should act up with ardour to the principles they profess.

I have already endeavoured to attract an attention to some of the strong pillars of our constitution, which form the safeguards of our liberties. These are,

1. One

1. One equal part of the National Sovereignty of this Nation compoſed of the People in the WHOLE HOUSE OF COMMONS.

2. The HABEAS Corpus Act, to preſerve us from wrongful impriſonment.

3. TRIAL BY JURY—to fecure us from unneceſſary profecution, and to protect us againſt injurious deciſions.

To them I ſhall now ſubjoin as inſeparably connected,

4. THE LIBERTY OF THE PRESS: and as far as I can collect from the general declarations lately publiſhed by aſſociations, what the mind of the people is moſt directed to,

5. The reviſion and ſimplification of the LAWS OF ENGLAND.

It

It is not my intention to enter into an historical detail of thefe feveral articles, of their origin and progrefs, or the means by which they have been gradually matured into elementary principles, forming, as they now do, the Conftitution. My defign is only to induce my fellow-citizens to give their own aid to perform thofe individual duties, on the punctual and faithful difcharge of which, the very prefervation of thofe bleffings which our conftitution diffufes among us fo materially depends. Thefe duties are fo important to every order of fociety and each department of the ftate, that no good citizen ought ever to decline them: yet, it is to be apprehended, that many of the abufes, or inconveniencies, now alledged to have crept into the practice of Government, may be fairly traced to our own indifference and neglect. As to a defign, that furely is impoffible; fince the very people who feel thefe alledged inconveniencies are to be found in each executive department of the state; and without whose knowledge and connivance, the encroachments now thought to be injurious, or to bear hard on the subject, could not possibly have continued. It is only by the assistance of the people that the responsible executive officers of the state are enabled to perform their important functions; and were they to withold their services, which common interest and honesty forbid, there must soon be an annihilation of the Government. Therefore, as the happiness and welfare of our country, and the domestic comforts we possess, absolutely depend on the faithful services of the people, my conscience tells me, I am not only justified, but that it is a duty which allegiance to the constitution demands, to offer the following observations.

SECTION

SECTION III.

HOUSE OF COMMONS.

IT has been already stated, "that nothing "but a mistaken infatuation can ever cause "us to forget, that out of three, the people "already possess one equal part of the na- "tional Sovereignty, through the medium "of their representatives the WHOLE "HOUSE OF COMMONS."—This is clearly, as great a share of the legislature as they can, consistent with their own happiness desire: and, when properly understood, their good sense cannot fail to convince them, that their true interests positively forbid more. This House of Commons is wholly composed of the people, whose free choice of its members individually, certified under their own act, is the only *fiat* under which the solemn oaths of allegiance, supremacy, and fidelity, can be adminstered; or any member admitted to a possible means of neglecting, or betraying the truſt of the people, or ſuffering any encroachment of the truſtees of the executive authority on the privileges of the ſubject. Nothing can conſtitute an act of the legiſlature which has not this conſent of the people: no tax or money can be levied: no military or naval armaments maintained,—nor mutiny and deſertion puniſhed, without ſuch conſent expreſsly and annually obtained: or, in other words, without their verdict as a national Jury of the People, " that it is right and ought to be done." And thus in every queſtion which can be agitated either in that houſe, or by the other branches of the legiſlature, this national jury muſt firſt approve the meaſure before it can be adopted: and if for argument ſake, we admit their judgment on any point to be erroneous, it muſt then undergo the rigid ſcrutiny of the other two co-ordinate branches, poſſeſſing alſo the diſtinct property of Juries which our conſtitution has wiſely deſigned,

to

to correct: so that by the vigilant exercise of this principle of each jealously checking and controuling the other, the individual branches possess as much power, as can be exercised with safety and benefit either to themselves, or to the whole. And hence my conclusions, that the true interest of the people of England positively forbids their possessing a larger share in the legislature than the happy construction of our present constitution allots them—" and so long
" as their House of Commons shall preserve
" its own dignity and independence, by
" faithfully adhering to the true principle
" and spirit of its institution, it is morally
" impossible that the rights of the people can
" ever be annihilated."—

This naturally induces the question, What is the end of this Institution, and in what does its principle and spirit consist? That it should be composed *wholly of the people*, and be a pure, unbiaſſed, and independent controul *in behalf of the people,* neither encroaching on, nor ſuffering encroachment; and, in its actions, neither knowing nor being known, by either of the other two eſtates; neither ſubmitting its conduct to influence, nor permitting interference; but, aſſiduouſly and unceaſingly watching, guarding, and preſerving this valuable and dignified ſpirit, founded on the natural rights of the people. It is the firſt duty of our Repreſentatives in their truſt, rigidly to preſerve this independent and well balanced order, under a fixed ſyſtem of diſtinct and jealous dignity, which forms repellants little ſhort of declared hoſtility towards the other two eſtates: for the moment they ſuffer this vital principle to be uſurped or infringed, the deſign of the inſtitution is ſubverted and diſordered; their independence and dignity are loſt; the whole fabric of the conſtitution, by the deſertion of its appointed guardians, is in danger of being ſacrificed; and

and under a continuance of mere form, the people no longer reprefented, are reduced to filent fubmiffion under arbitrary authority.

Thus, I conceive, the end of this Inftitution is, a general guardianfhip for the people againft arbitrary power, as dictated by wicked, tyrannical, and fanguinary ufurpations, during the fuperftition and ignorance of paft ages; and which our patriotic anceftors determined it wife, pofitively, and for ever, to prohibit, by eftablifhing an Houfe of Reprefentatives with power, not only competent to its own functions, but qualified, as every body knows, by withholding pecuniary fupplies, to dictate to the other two Eftates, whenever the condition of the State fhall demand it.—And, on the other hand, all the acts of this branch of the Legiflature being affented to by the other two (provided they are fuch as do not militate againft the conftitution),

are

are binding on the people; and, thenceforward, it becomes their duty, rigidly, faithfully, and implicitly to fubfcribe obedience, and to render their perfonal fervices for the accomplifhment of the compact. Hence, the importance of this Houfe to the People, and the neceffity of the free, and judicious, choice of its members: hence, the fource of that jealoufy with which their conduct is fo accurately fcrutinized; and of the expedience of fuch vigilance being inceffant in its operation; hence too fhould be decifion of judgment; fevere and unrelenting refentment towards fuch of their national Reprefentatives as fail in their duty.

How far our Houfe of Reprefentatives is at prefent, what the fpirit of the conftitution demands, or whether it requires an immediate Reform, is a fubject, of which I fhall not enter into minute difcuffion, as that would be encroaching on a department already engaging

ing the moſt diſtinguiſhed characters of this kingdom, whoſe brilliant talents, and political integrity, can only be equalled by their ardent zeal for the public good; and by that exemplary moderation with which they proceed in aſſuming a duty of ſuch eſſential moment to the liberties of the people; and which too had been before moſt ſolemnly promiſed by others, yet neverthelefs, precipitately abandoned, as ſoon as the means were obtained of fulfilling the engagements they had entered into.

On this point therefore, I ſhall only add, my mite of applauſe to the " FRIENDS OF THE PEOPLE," for their honeſt and aſſiduous ſervices in the preſervation and maintenance of our happy conſtitution; nor is it a ſmall ſtep towards their ſuccefs, that the elective franchiſe poſſeſſes one advantage over all other property, that its benefits are not leſſened by being diffuſed to plurality

of

of objects; for no one man can be injured in his privilege of voting by its being extended to another. By thus multiplying the right, and by limiting elections to one and the same day throughout the kingdom, a fair prospect is afforded of diminishing contest, of annihilating bribery and corruption, and other undue influence, and of satisfying the public mind, that our HOUSE OF COMMONS actually is—what it ought to be,—the REAL and GENUINE REPRESENTATION of the PEOPLE.

SECTION IV.

HABEAS CORPUS ACT, TO PRESERVE US FROM WRONGFUL IMPRISONMENT.

ARBITRARY imprisonment has, in all ages, been a summary mode of disposing of individuals, whether obnoxious through popularity, or any other cause. It has been

been found convenient to promote the dark purposes of men perverting discretionary authority, into ministerial intrigue; and for the most part finds a veil in a blind submission to general confidence. The history of all states furnishes but too many examples of so nefarious a practice. And this general hostility against human liberty has pointed out the necessity of providing strong entrenchments to secure it. Our ancestors, afflicted and tortured by the severities of oppression, were early roused to seek a remedy, and they have left us the valuable privilege of Habeas Corpus, as the glorious monument of a triumph over despotism. From that moment it has been decided, that the personal liberty of Britons should no longer be at the disposal of discretionary power. It is, therefore, our duty to preserve this glorious restitution made us for all the blood and treasure expended in the contest. Our laws so amply afford us the means of doing

so

so, that no causes, short of that extreme necessity created by an actual foreign invasion, —or internal rebellion, in which the safety of the state is likely to be shaken, can at any time justify its suspension. There is at present not a shadow of the appearance of any intestine disturbance; to assert otherwise, would be a libel on the people; and the grossest calumny.

State necessity never dictates but on a principle of self preservation:—to remedy or provide against existing evils, not to create them; nor can any state be interested in the destruction of itself. The Liberty of Britain is her only basis founded on Magna Charta: and any doctrine to persuade Britons, that the Constitution would stand when Liberty was destroyed, would be an insult. That Liberty must be lasting and immutable; alike sacred to all men, but more especially so to those in power, who are purposely placed

placed on duty to guard it even from the breath of invasion :—nor would Britons endure a law, rendering it liable to instability, or such occasional modification as the crooked policy of any existing administration might capriciously determine: if it were so, this only distinction between a free state and a land of slavery, might soon be removed, and Liberty reduced to a mere insulting password for treacherous imposition. In this light, the privilege of Habeas Corpus must be more zealously guarded against contingent modification than any other, because more liable to fall a sacrifice to the inroads of power. The other component parts of the Constitution possessing repellants, contribute to support each other against injury or invasion: but the Habeas Corpus stands, as it were, single and detached, and finds no assistance from the rest but in the precarious issue of the law; after a mischievous assault has been sustained.

The fufpenfion of the Habeas Corpus act, is an explicit declaration, that the falutary law which preferves perfonal liberty againft wrongful imprifonment, fhall be temporarily repealed; and that any citizen may be deprived of his Liberty at the difcretion of an officiating magiftrate; and, however flagrant the injuftice, without the power of reforting to the Habeas Corpus for relief, or as the means of knowing the offence alledged againft him.

It is true there is no appearance of fuch a declaration at prefent: but a partial fufpenfion has been in agitation when it was wrong and unneceffary. For if a falfe alarm is to occafion a diminution of our privileges, what may not be juftly apprehended, fhould a convulfion take place in the ftate, through unwife, erroneous, or unfuccefsful meafures, in times too portending events of which no human judgment can forefee the end?—Any partial fufpenfion wantonly refolved on, can only

only foretell a general one;—the next gradation would be a total abrogation. It is our indifpenfable duty to avert this. It fhould too be the firft care of our agents in parliament to guard not that alone, but all our liberties, with vigilance and unceafing jealoufy. We depute them to reprefent us with limited powers, and thefe are exprefsly reftricted to our benefit. We have no where given them an authority, either directly or implied, to deprive us of our franchifes*. It was with fevere ftruggles they were

---

* Blackftone. Vol. I. p. 161, Ninth Edition, fpeaking of Parliament—" It can change or create afrefh, even the " Conftitution of the Kingdom, and of Parliaments them-" felves, as was done by the act of Union, and the feveral " Statutes of triennial and feptennial Elections." As the celebrated author of the Commentaries was too conftitutional to infinuate a charge of public coercion or ufurpation againft any of the three Eftates, he could only mean to veft fuch extraordinary powers in the parliament, certain that they would never be enforced but at the exprefs inftance and unequivocal fenfe of the nation at large; and muft wholly concentre in that exclufive privilege which enables the People, by their Houfe of Commons, to dictate to the other two Eftates.

acquired, and our laws have ordained, that they shall not be easily parted with. This can only be done by the general and unanimous consent, not only of the whole people of these united Kingdoms, but by the concurrence of the other two co-ordinate Estates, equally the trustees of the People. To suspend the Habeas Corpus unnecessarily, therefore, would be to betray us, and disgrace themselves. — It would be imposing a most serious and alarming grievance; and one that the last necessity only, arising from some public convulsion, could justify; a necessity which does not at present exist. Are the good people in a state of Rebellion, as has been most wickedly insinuated, who daily manifest their loyalty by open and declaratory acts? Or are we invaded by a foreign enemy?

In order to be enabled to act up to the principles of veneration which we profess for the

the Conſtitution, we ought not to ſuffer any indifference for it, under a blind confidence in men, infenſibly to poſſeſs us *.— It belongs to us, to ſee that they perform their functions. And it may be confidered as a misfortune, that the generality of the world, pleaſed with indolent ſecurity, are ſatisfied to partake of the benefits of ſociety

---

* The Decemviri of Rome were choſen from among the moſt diſpaſſionate, unambitious citizens, to compile a code of laws for the uſe of the people, and were entruſted with abſolute power over the Commonwealth. In private life they were men of auſtere morals, rigid integrity, and mild diſpoſitions; and it was with much difficulty, and not without apparent reluctance that they could be prevailed on to accept the truſt: yet ſoon afterwards, inebriated with power and the advantages of office, they openly threw off the maſk, and became ſo odious for their tyranny, that in the third year after their creation, the people were ſo highly exaſperated as to demand them from the Senate in order to burn them alive."

This was no more than the ordinary effect of a too ready confidence in their intentions and ſervices, and a blind reliance on their integrity and moderation; and it teaches us at leaſt, that we ought not always to ſleep, becauſe we have a ſtationary watch on duty.

without any participation of the hazards and services by which they are acquired, or interesting themselves in the means by which they are to be preserved. This indolent security and unsuspecting confidence, has proved one of the sharpest thorns in the side of human happiness. For power not less the instrument of general mischief than the guardian of public benefit, should be considered only as the sacred stock of the community; and even when most necessary, but temporarily delegated to individuals for a special service; and like arms distributed among citizens for the occasional defence of a state, to be returned as soon as a specific duty has been performed. In a crisis like the present, when it is difficult to assume an alternative between civil confusion and abject humiliation, it becomes the duty of every good citizen and well-wisher to the Constitution, to watch the moment of error or danger; and when we behold measures adopted
which

which threaten to break down the ſtrongeſt barriers of human ſecurity, it behoves us to conſult and aſſociate for general protection, as the only means of averting convulſion.

It has been obſerved, that when we depute our Repreſentatives to parliament, we do not inveſt them with an authority to diſpoſe of or even to weaken our privileges. Were that authority to be granted in any inſtance, it might be practiced in all; and that conſtitution we ſo much revere, and the Liberties emanating therefrom, might in one day be ſacrificed to deſign or neglect, and this region of freedom, be converted into a land of ſlavery and deſpotiſm. While the Habeas Corpus retains its virtue, we ſleep in ſecurity: if not happy and contented, who can we reproach when we feel ourſelves placed beyond the reach of arbitrary diſpoſitions? But, this act once ſuſpended (which may be ſeriouſly apprehended ſhould we be hurried into Hoſtilities with
France)

France) who is secure? Or what man can rise in the morning and be certain, that he shall not pass the ensuing night in a dungeon, or within the walls of an inquisition, secreted from his family, not knowing where or how to call for relief? What father of a family is there to be found, whose chearful fire-side might not be suddenly turned into a scene of horror, shrieks, and mourning; their natural protector torn from his endearing station?—

The extreme of necessity can only warrant so violent an outrage on the constitution. Let us, therefore, admonish our Representatives in parliament, and recommend to them, as they value their own liberties, and revere our Constitution; as they regard their duty, and bear in remembrance the solemn oaths which enabled them to enter on their functions; and as they may expect to receive the future confidence of their Constituents,

not

not to confent on any confideration fhort of the laft neceflity, that the Habeas Corpus Act fhould be even for a moment fufpended.

The right of Electors to inftruct their reprefentatives in parliament has been often debated, though the doubt of its exiftence muft affuredly be unfounded. Elfe, what means the privilege of a free-poftage?— Whence its origin? But that the correfpondence on the duties of their deputation, fhould not be fubject to impediment? Were it otherwife, how could Members conduct themfelves, who are probably ftrangers in the places they reprefent, and whofe avocations in life have never afforded them the opportunity of attaining a knowledge of thofe particular interefts, which it is the object of their miffion to promote? An elegant writer whofe principles and philanthropy are as fuperior to fufpicion, as to praife, fpeaking of our Houfe of Reprefentatives, lays it down as an axiom, "that the virtue, fpirit, and ef- "fence of it confifts in its being the exprefs "image of the feelings of the nation." What does this import, but, that, in the true fenfe and fpirit of a delegated truft, our feelings are to be their feelings; our interefts, their interefts; and our inftructions, their particular duty? Let us not then, at any time, be deterred from offering either ufeful inftruction, or feafonable admonition; or from motives of cenfurable delicacy, fee them run wildly into error, or extremes; and, in the exercife of their functions, act with as much indifference towards their Conftituents, as if they were treating about the private property of an eftate, the live ftock, and all its appurtenances. Every reprefentative, who knows his duty, and contemns not the hand from whence he derived his commiffion, will court our aid, and pride himfelf on his obedience and his fervices. And, I truft, every good citizen

zen who venerates the Conftitution, will unite with me in deprecating any injury to this bulwark of our perfonal liberty, fince his tranquillity and fafety are more or lefs involved in it; and fince the throne of thefe realms is never fo fecurely eftablifhed, as when fupported by public freedom, and voluntary affection.

SECTION

SECTION V.

TRIAL BY JURY,
TO SECURE US FROM UNNECESSARY PROSECUTION, AND TO PROTECT US AGAINST INJURIOUS DECISIONS.

WHILST the eloquent and undismayed DEFENDER of the LIBERTY of the PRESS shall continue to plead:—Whilst the faithful FRIEND OF THE PEOPLE, by defending our rights, continues to strengthen our Constitution; to enlighten, and to charm his cotemporaries into the emulation of his example; and, whilst we mentally contemplate that glorious monument, erected for the benefit of the people at the shrine of virtue, on which stands inscribed,

The REDEMPTION

OF THE

RIGHTS OF THE PEOPLE,

FROM LONG INSIDIOUS USURPATION,

THE PROUD REWARD

OF

INTEGRITY UNSUSPECTED,

AND

TALENTS UNSURPASSED,

TRIAL

TRIAL by JURY, though long familiar to the willing ear of Britons, muſt continue to generate new veneration, even among them, and to impreſs diſtant nations with its purity, dignity, and importance; nay, even poſterity will be induced to rival each other in admiration, until the iron arm of ſome new found tyranny ſhall deface its beauty, or time ſhall be no more!

The tribute of applauſe being paid to the reſtorers of our long alienated right—" the " Power of juries to decide on both Law " and Fact, in proſecutions for Libel;"— and this brilliant conqueſt recorded in our hearts; our next object of conſideration is, the means of preſerving and handing the ſacred pledge down to poſterity, as perfect and untainted, as, in its preſent purified ſtate, we now receive it.

Beautiful as we behold trial by jury, in theory;

theory; and competent as it is to afford us all the bleffings and advantages it promifes; yet without our farther aid and fupport, even this alluring fabric cannot long withftand the infidious attack—the undermining fap, which defigning men may, and, in all human probability, *will* attempt againft it. We ought, therefore, not only to be thankful for its attainment, but gratitude requires that we fhould deferve it by our conduct.

Had Mr. Fox's Act been obtained thirty years ago, or had its principles been underftood, and firmly acted up to, as became the duty of a People tenacious of their birthrights and privileges, how much poignant diftrefs, undeferved punifhment, exorbitant fine, and loathfome imprifonment, would have been unfelt—how many unhappy Victims had not, in that period, fallen under thefe fevere afflictions—a period, poffibly of more importance to the Liberty of the Prefs,

the

the ſtate of civil government, and the general diſſemination of knowledge, than any of the ſame duration within the annals of Hiſtory? Though this may be a reflection more particularly applicable to men in the habit of committing their thoughts to the preſs, it is not, however, of ſmall importance for us to conſider the wounds which civilization has ſuſtained, as a means of preventing them in future.

Some attentions and ſupport this tranſcendant fabric muſt ever require; not the leaſt of which is an occaſional attendance to ſerve on juries. This is ſo eaſy to individuals, ſo reaſonable in itſelf, that a good citizen will bluſh at any remiſſneſs of which he may be conſcious.

Judge Blackſtone has told us, " that it is " the tranſcendent privilege of every Engliſh- " man, that he cannot be affected in either

" his

" his Property, his Liberty, or his Perſon,
" but by *the unanimous conſent of twelve of his*
" *Neighbours and Equals.*" What benign comfort, what ſecurity of Liberty, Perſon, and Property, does the abſtract impreſſion of this doctrine imperceptibly inſtil into our minds; and how ſuperior does it teach *us to value ourſelves* over the inhabitants of other regions of the world, where trial by jury is unknown! Happy had now been diſtracted France, inhabited by twenty-five millions of people, could a Frenchman formerly, like ourſelves, have ſaid—" my Liberty, my Per-
" ſon, my Property are ſacred, until at leaſt
" twelve Frenchmen can be found unani-
" mouſly of opinion, that fact and law
" demand that I ſhould ſubmit to a depriva-
" tion of them." If, then, the preſent miſeries of Europe may be attributed to the want of that formidable rampart of the people's rights, the trial by jury, which I moſt cordially believe :—If we behold deſpotiſm
exerciſed

exercifed in every ftate throughout the world where trial by jury has not erected a ftandard; and, if even in our own, where it is known " to be almoft coeval with the coun-
" try, and its very inftitution to have given
" birth to an imperfect conftitution;" we find, that the mind of man, naturally prone to tyranny and ufurpation, had, in the courfe of time, fo completely undermined its very effence, as almoft to have reduced an empannelled jury to the mere fkeleton of abject obedience to the expounder of the law.—How glorious then ought to be the exultation of Britons; and how perfonally grateful fhould they feel towards their fellow-citizens, whofe integrity, eloquence, and undifmayed perfeverance, have reftored to us this bleffing; with the fplendor and purity of its original intention!!—Such feelings fhould convince us, that it is beneath the dignity of our character to fhew an indifference, or a difinclination to ferve on juries; evafions from which

which have been to my own knowledge, so frequent, as even to have afforded the opportunity and specious plea for those usurpations of which we have hitherto had reason to complain.

To be satisfied that this is not an occasional opinion, or some newly adopted principle, I hope it will not be deemed impertinent to assert, that ever since I have attained the age of qualification, I have never declined acting either as a grand or petty juror according to the citations I may have received; and though for many years entrusted with important public duties, I have never suffered either those, or my own private concerns, of whatever nature they may have been, serve as pleas for the evasion of this my first duty as an Englishman.

Next to the disinclination of serving on juries, is another evil which has lately appeared

peared of no lefs dangerous tendency: I mean, that of the voluntary, though unintentional difqualifications, to act as jurors, by means of fignatures to parochial declarations, moft loyally intended, and fo far laudable; but certainly, in many particulars, infringing violently on our privileges; and even fatally propagating thofe evils, which a miftaken zeal might have hoped to diffipate. It did not perhaps at firft occur, that fuch combinations violated the conftitution by the erection of tribunals, inquifitions, and inquifitors, as odious in name every where, as arbitrary and illegal in practice. Who would not fhudder, if but for a moment, confidered as an inquifitor? And yet, how many have voluntarily affumed that office! I will endeavour to illuftrate this by adverting to fome of the leading points of the declarations in queftion.

1. One

1. One of the objects is declared to be, to aid the civil authority in quelling riots, tumults, &c. Is not this acknowledging, that the Executive Government is either inadequate to its functions, or that they are so badly administered, as to want the necessity of aid? And, is it not an assurance of the existence of riot and tumult; to the truth of which, your declarations and subscriptions are pledged. I must affirm it as a truth, that the powers possessed by the Executive Trustees of this country, are more than competent to their duties; and, were it otherwise, I hope they are not so unwise to acknowledge such insufficiency by the acceptance of any such offers. To pretend that the people are riotous and tumultuous, is a foul imputation—a gross libel on them; and every one who loves the good order which prevails, and is satisfied of the competency of the Executive Government to discharge its functions, must consider any declaration

declaration to the contrary as deserving severe reprobation.

2. Denunciations are issued against the circulators of all such publications as have a tendency to sedition, and rewards are held out to informers.—Here again, zeal has strangely exposed prudence; and a mischief is propagated by a blind endeavour to avert it. Just returned from the triumph of a late victory in establishing the uncontrouled liberty of the press, by an act supported by the suffrages of the WHOLE NATION save THREE OPPOSING VOICES, there is now a precipitate determination to violate it; and a virtual declaration that the nation shall not have that privilege. And, instead of the three individuals who officially declared their hostility to it; and, therefore, had the eyes of the whole nation directed

to their conduct, endeavours are now used so to multiply its enemies, that its true friends may chance to be borne down and suffocated in the confusion, as will appear;

3. When citizens are called on to unite in this assumed jurisdiction, with design to prosecute, punish, reward, &c. Is it then meant to be declared that the established laws of the empire, which are so numerous as to give employment and fortunes to one hundred thousand men engaged in the profession, are, nevertheless incompetent to punish the offences of which cognizance is thus unconstitutionally assumed; and as if there were no other jurisdiction? Under this impression, every man is qualified and capable of becoming a vile corrupt informer and an incorrupt judge of libel and sedition; and in the very same breath, again disqualified from acting either as judge, juror, or witness, by summarily pre-judging and pre-determining offences

ces even before they have been committed. Thus, unwarily, all the pains are taken which ingenious men can take (and greater ingenuity was never more requisite) to undo these extraordinary doings, by requiring every body to associate; so that the probability is, that we may soon have offences to arraign without an unprejudiced magistrate before whom to arraign them; and offenders to try, without an impartial jury to decide.—Or, if otherwise, as all good citizens, not foreseeing or reflecting on the consequences of these implied evils, will have united in associations which have for their object the pure support of the king and constitution; by rashly and injudiciously mingling the discordant principles of jarring and restless politics with professions of loyalty,—by a poisonous composition of loyalty, sedition, and libel,—and by a treasonable interference with the laws of the state, we shall leave only such of the suspicious and disaffected who may not find employment

employment as informers, to perform the diftinct duties of magiftrate and juror; and thus become the fole arbiters and difpofers of all the informations, libels, feditions, riots, and tumults, which the influence and enticement of profered rewards, collufion and fecret combination may excite.

4. Neither are extraordinary denunciations againft productions of feditious or libellous tendency, calculated to obtain the end which is promifed. So far from correcting the mifchievous impreffion, which fuch productions are admitted to be capable of making on the public mind; by fulminatory denunciations, it is avowed that there is no ability to over-rule their influence and reafoning; and, therefore, refort is to be had to violent fuppreffion and fummary condemnation. Thefe denunciations are fo general and undefined, that it is impoffible to fay precifely what doctrines may or may not be the marked

ed objects of indignation and resentment.—
If they go to question the scheme of our constitution and government, I am decidedly of opinion, that the easiest and most efficacious way would have been to expose the poison which the publications in question might chance to contain; and to instruct uninformed Britons in the principles of the constitution. It is not the constitution that is bad, but the extravagance and intrigues of the people in power, which deform its appearance, and render it hideous to such as see through a distant medium; and perhaps only judge of it by the payment of taxes. And this, possibly, there may be a greater desire of suppressing, than all the libels and seditions, as well those which have as those which have not appeared. Doubts of our constitution can only proceed from want of knowledge; while to explain what the constitution really is, would be the infallible means of making those who live under it sensible of the blessings they derive from it; and

of increasing their attachment. Such is the design of this address; and if it should only tend to render one misled citizen a convert to the solid blessings we possess, the object will be answered and my time amply requited. And here I shall conclude my observations on trial by jury with a solemn exhortation to my countrymen,—to emulate each other in fulfilling their duty, as Jurors, with alacrity, patience and cheerfulness, as the certain means of protecting each other against oppression when attempted; of preserving the dignity of our laws when offended; and as the infallible means, of maintaining the King and the People in that uninterrupted affection and harmony which are the reciprocal object and true interest of both.

SECTION

SECTION VI.

THE LIBERTY OF THE PRESS.

THIS object is fo infeparably connected, and interwoven with the general liberties, and welfare of mankind, as to command our moſt active and lively protection. The liberty of the preſs is indeed the grand cement and organ of fociety;—the faithful channel by which all good works are promulgated, and bad ones cenfured and expoſed. It is the induſtrious and indefatigable agent for the inſtant circulation of particular intelligence, and for the deliberate diſſemination of general knowledge: the infallible fupport of the honeſt, and fafe refort of the injured. It is the jealous avenger of wrongs; the vigilant guardian of rectitude. It diſtributes puniſhment to vice and rewards to virtue. It is an impenetrable ſhield

againſt

against oppression, and the soul of integrity.—It is, as it were, the discerning eye of the public, and respects and distinguishes men as their conduct intrinsically merits. It is the sincere friend of freedom. The implacable enemy of slavery. The intellectual mirror of the universe designed to reflect happiness on mankind, in which every man has an inherent property. And it is so inseparably attached and affianced to trial by jury, that they are the immutable support of each other; and so long as jurors support the press, the press will support jurors. It thus becomes the soul of all our personal liberties; and the national safeguard, without which the dogmatical mandate of an ambitious minister might be rendered the sole arbiter of civil government and freedom; and that constitution which we so enthusiastically venerate, soon become a dead letter.

Such are the virtues and diffusive properties

ties of the prefs: fuch the benefits it profeſſes to propagate throughout the world, to the unſhackled exerciſe of which is committed the enviable conſtitution of England! How rigid, then, ſhould we not be in maintaining and preſerving this univerſal vehicle of human wiſdom, in which the happineſs of the world and of generations yet unborn are ſo eſſentially involved! With what determination and ardour ſhould we not inſiſt on its free uſe; and, how reſentful ought we not to be on any abuſe likely to endanger it!—

Here again, my friends, let us pauſe, and unite in paying the grateful tribute of ſenſibility:—Let us hail the GUARDIAN GENIUS OF BRITAIN, to whoſe ſplendid talents we are indebted for this lately acquired ornament—the corner ſtone of that heavenly attribute, to which nature gave exiſtence, but ſelected him to emanate its virtue

tue and to interpret its intelligence, to the glorious purpose of encreasing the happiness of mankind!—Neither let us forget to applaud the valuable services which in defiance of every discouragement and encreasing difficulty, the cause derived from the long and unremitted exertions of the celebrated orator of the English bar, and which so forcibly contributed to its success!—

As I have given my thoughts on the important use of the press, I shall offer some observations on the abuse of it. I am well aware that so extensive a blessing cannot be diffused in a world composed of human beings, without carrying along with it the misfortune of partial evil: yet, where much must necessarily be imperfect, we should look only to the preponderance of the scale; and while that is in the favour of virtue, we ought not to be discontented. With regard to the evil, good sense should teach us, that violent coercion

cannot

cannot be the effectual mode of repressing it. Silence and contempt are the only weapons with which abuses of the press in general should be combated, and which never fail to inflict a mortal blow. Should, however, the depravity of the times so much sway the minds of men as to induce them to circulate publications with a view to excite the people to resist the civil magistrate, or to obstruct the execution of the existing laws, such publications are certainly deserving the censure of society, and the seasonable punishment of the law:—but, the degree of that punishment and that censure should, in all cases, be determined by society in its two-fold delegation of juries: I mean that the offences of the press, called libels,—like every outrage of the laws of society, should be subject to a similar process. This, I conceive, must have been the original meaning of our constitution. Whereas, such offences of the Press as are deemed obnoxious to government,

ment, are now profecuted on *ex-officio* information by the attorney general, who is an officer of the crown, *wherever* or *whenever* he may be *ex-officio* inftructed to carry his procefs on iffue direct, before a petty jury only.—So that the grand jury, that palladium of the liberties of England, " formed " from among ourfelves to fecure us from un- " fair or unneceffary profecution," is in this inftance fuperceded. Nor do I conceive the alteration which I here fuggeft, at all oppofed by the conftitutional principles of Sir William Blackftone, who fpeaking of *ex-officio* profecutions (vol. 4. page 308) defcribes them to be, " fuch enormous mifdemeanors
" as peculiarly tend to difturb or endanger
" the King's government, or to moleft or
" affront him in the regular difcharge of the
" royal functions: for offences fo high and
" dangerous in the punifhment or preven-
" tion of which a moment's delay would
" be fatal, the law has given to the
" crown

" crown the power of an immediate pro-
" fecution, without waiting for any pre-
" vious application to any other tribunal."
Here Sir William Blackstone clearly cannot
mean promiscuously to include prosecutions
for every description of Libel, fortuitously
and constructively arising in " the free dif-
" cussion and examination of the principles
" of civil government, and of all matter of
" public opinion."

An entire alteration, or some modification of the present practice, was never more
necessary than at this time of innovation
and unsettled opinion. The protection of
the subject against interested suspicion and
unprovoked oppression, is the more urgent-
ly called for, as since the establishment of
the associations to reward informers against
the circulation of productions of seditious
tendency, &c. upwards of one hundred
informations, (as I have been told, though I
should

should hope the number is somewhat exaggerated) have been preferred to the attorney general for *ex officio* prosecution; even during the sitting of the GRAND JURY OF MIDDLESEX, in the centre of this metropolis; before whom two or three informations did however find their way; as it was naturally conceived to be the constitutional jurisdiction of the kingdom *.

---

* The time for prosecutions of libels, like those on penal statutes, ought to be limited: for, if the prosecution is not immediate, the evil, which, in the first instance, a jury might have arrested, is circulated beyond that reach which is the object of preventative punishment. And it is doubtful, whether silence for a reasonable time does not even sanction a libel. Nor, is the mischief of long delay at all confined to the original work, since every vender in its propagated state becomes unwarily involved. It is to be hoped the associations for rewarding informers on this subject, do not mean their denunciations to extend to venders of copies, before the Country, in the capacity of a Jury, have condemned the original: but, as I have before observed, it is almost impossible to define, either the objects of their disapprobation, the parties likely to be exempt from their anger, or the intended extent of so deformed a jurisdiction.

Committing

Committing this suggestion to the judgment of abler men, I shall conclude the subject with an admonitory address to some of the new formed associations; in the hope of awakening them to a sense of that unconstitutional conduct into which their intemperate zeal has plunged them. As free Citizens of the same state with myself, I trust they will receive, without passion or prejudice, what I presume to offer.

The professed object of your associations was to declare an attachment to the king and constitution; and, thus far, the institution could not be too much commended. This was all that the particular exigence required; this you accomplished. And had you rested there, your conduct would have claimed the unanimous support of the nation. But, this laudable object was no sooner obtained, than you corrupted its purity; and either overzealous, or ignorant, or regardlefs of the means by which the defired end was to be maintained, you adulterated your loyalty by mingling with it difcordant politics; and undermined the conftitution, by direct attempts to deftroy the very foul of thofe liberties, which are its beft fupport.

By correfpondence with each other, and by circulating fuch prints only as tend to fupport your own unfcrutinized doctrines: by condemning indifcriminately all others as " libellous, or feditious, exciting to riot " or tumult," you every where fet the moft fubtile engines in motion fo far to deftroy the liberty of the prefs, as to referve the exclufive abufe of it to yourfelves. And you ftill expect that thefe corrupted channels will poffefs fufficient virtue to render every man a convert to the principles they promulgate. The people of a free ftate are however not to be dragooned into affection and

and reverence for such opinions of " sedition " and libel, riot, and tumult," as you may wish to establish.

Be assured, that the liberty of the press, the " implacable enemy to slavery" is too firmly rooted in the heart of the world, to be shaken by any such sacrilegious efforts; that the happiness of mankind is too deeply involved in its preservation to withhold their most active faculties in its defence; and in branding its opponents with all the opprobrium attached to declared enemies of the human race. Be advised, and avert farther reprehension from this " jealous avenger of wrongs."— Retire from impending disgrace; and purify your adulterated loyalty. Remember, that the liberties of these kingdoms are the sole and infallible support of the constitution; and that all societies tending to undermine it are treasonably hostile.—— Hasten then, though late, to restore yourfelves to the dignity of citizens of a free ftate.

SECTION VII.

THE REVISION AND SIMPLIFICATION OF THE LAWS OF ENGLAND.

" *LAW is nothing but REASON REFINED, or REASON*
" *REGULATED; the refults of Counfel and Wifdom,*
" *after long and mature deliberation.*"
HAKEWELL—MOD. TENENDI PARLIAMENTI.

AS the good order of fociety is the fupport of every ftate, fo good laws form the effence of fociety. Free governments more efpecially inculcate thefe maxims.—The knowledge too of the laws fhould be the effential ftudy of individuals, fince it is impoffible for them to be obeyed, or fociety to be undifturbed by infringements, whilft they are either unknown, or not thoroughly underftood. Where the evil of doubtful laws exifts, it is morally impoffible that a people can be free from error. And hence arifes the expedience of their fimplification. Laws fhould be reduced to the underftandings of the moft uninformed, who, in all populous ftates, comprife the great mafs of the inhabitants.— The object of philofophical enquiry is the happinefs and profperity of the human race. But, what can fo materially affect that happinefs as an ignorance of the means by which it is to be promoted and fecured; an ignorance that progreffively encreafes with population; by which fociety gradually lofes the benefit of legal advantages, in proportion as her exigencies encreafe; and the fame caufes too which fwell the evil, augment the difficulty of the remedy.

On thefe principles it is my wifh to fuggeft the neceffity of a revifion of the laws of England. That they are wife and good; have
been

been infpired by virtue, and framed by integrity, are truths univerfally acknowledged. But they are known only to a few, and perhaps not perfectly comprehended by any. They are by time, incident, and the precautions of paft ages to protect perfonal liberty and fecure property, become fo extenfive, that the life of man is too fhort to obtain a perfect acquaintance with them. A fact continually exemplified by frequent declarations from the bench, and the doubts of the moft able, learned, and profound lawyers. Hence, it is evident that civil law, which fhould be open to the underftanding of all, is become an abftrufe fcience, never wholly acquired by any; and as far as attainable, entirely confined to the fmall circle of profeffional men, become fuch by expenfive education. Another evil is, that our code abounds with obfolete ftatutes, which prove ancient and modern practice to be fo much at variance, as to dictate the neceffity

either

either of expunging the one, or correcting the other. Nor is the influence of thefe evils confined to the profeſſion of the law; it extends to each department of the ſtate; and every corner of the conſtitution is more or leſs ſubject to it. We ſo often ſee the law called forth to interpret the conſtitution, that they are virtually at the mercy and diſpoſal of the few profeſſional gentlemen whom ſucceſs may have created general arbiters and referees, with competency to decide what is or is not law and conſtitution. It is far from my intention to inſinuate, that they are either unfit for the truſt—or have ſacrificed their duty to their intereſt:— but I am of opinion, that it is of too ſerious import to be ſo confided:—too ſacred to be depoſited with any but the people at large; and that it can never be too vigilantly watched or too delicately handled.—I contend, therefore, that the law and conſtitution ſhould be clearly and diſtinctly defined, and so perfectly intelligible as to admit of explanation by every man who either can or cannot read; that whoever becomes liable to the penalties of infringement, should at least know how to avoid them; and that those who are aggrieved in that property, the loss of which probably may precede the the loss of personal liberty, should possess the means of legal defence in pleading their own cause if they chuse it, without the necessity of ruining themselves by the resources of precarious technical assistance. Such was the ancient rule of these kingdoms, and, without doubt it still prevails in remote parts of them; and, as, in this we may trace the origin of trial by jury, the difficulty of restoring this practice will appear less formidable. Trial by jury, originated in the assemblage of elders and neighbours of the same vicinage where questions arose, to hear grievances and to judge as their experience might direct: and here parties were confronted, each relating

ing his own tale in the language of unlettered fimplicity. This was the ufage in their own vicinage; and, when carried from home to fair or market, (the general extent of their *foreign* concerns), if in their dealings, any difputes or difagreements arofe, they immediately reforted to the court of *piedfpoudres* (or dufty feet) at which the lord's fteward, prefided; that term implying that their differences muft be frefh, and, therefore moft likely to be divefted of deceit, falfehood, or impofition.—Thus, it may be feen, that trial by jury, which originated more in neceffity than defign,—" is almoft
" coeval with the country, and that its very
" inftitution gave birth to an imperfect
" conftitution."

But, even in more modern times, and long fubfequent to the difcovery of printing, the fame cuftom of parties pleading for themfelves continued, until printed ftatutes, statutes, introduced in a *foreign* language, became so multiplied that individuals were no longer competent to conduct their own causes; and it was this confusion and incompetence that introduced scientific pleading. Hence, we may judge, how practicable it would now be, so far to revert to the ancient custom, as for individuals unattended by counsel, to relate their own wrongs before a jury of liberal Englishmen; and for that jury to decide thereon. If, then, this be possible, where lies the objection? The impracticability indeed can only exist in the number and abstruseness of our statutes; for, the people are not less competent to relate, or juries to hear and understand, than formerly. The advantages of the press have been diffused to all classes of society; for even those who cannot read, have greater opportunities of hearing; and, consequently, the general understanding of the people must be proportionably enlarged:

enlarged: fo that it is evident complainants as well as juries poffefs ftronger powers of relating, comprehending, and deciding, than in more fimple ages. Another advantage, which this practice would indifputably poffefs, is, that cafes would be perfectly genuine, and lefs liable to that miftatement, which is the inevitable confequence of a recital running through many channels. An individual, who has a cafe at law, muft, by the prefent mode, firft relate it to his Solicitor—the Solicitor to Counfel—and the Counfel to the Jury. In each of thefe ftages the original ftory lofes fomething of its energy: and the man who ftarts with a good caufe, ultimately finds its fubftance fo wafted or evaporated during a circuitous progrefs, as to leave only its fhadow to be decided on*.

---

* A perfon neceffitated to appeal to the laws of his country, is firft obliged to add to the eftablifhment of his expence, that of a Solicitor, for whofe time and fervices he

Of this, if prefent at the trial, he has too frequently the mortification to be fenfible, and he is almoft the only one debarred from interference. Whereas, had he been allowed to tell his own ftory to the jury, this could never have happened; confequently, he retires indignantly, and with forrow from the fcene, difcontented with

he muft pay, as well as for thofe of his clerks. He is next alfo obliged to pay this Solicitor for the employment of two Barrifters and their clerks. And, when his caufe is brought into Court, he muft then contribute to the maintenance of the officers of that Court. All this time he is unceafingly contributing to the purfe of the ftate by ftamps, paper duties, &c. Terrified with this burthenfome expence, he will be ftrongly prompted to afk himfelf, how long it is likely to laft. He now finds, that all the preceding grievances are comparatively trifling, and unworthy his uneafinefs; for, irretrievably involved, he perceives the caufe is no longer his own, but entirely at the difpofal of his Solicitor, as are poffibly all his fortunes along with it. His intereft indeed is become fecondary only; and having no claim on the perfonal affection of his Solicitor, his reliance againft impending deftruction is folely on the ability and refponfibility, which may attach on the profeffional character he has employed.

the

the law, and poffibly ruined by its decifion.

When a man muft have recourfe to the
laws of the fociety in which he lives, by the
fimplicity of thofe laws he ought, at leaft, to
be enabled to fee his way through them;
inftead of involving himfelf, as at prefent he
inevitably muft, in a dark inextricable
labyrinth.

The fupport of all the liberal part of the
profeffion may at leaft be looked for, whofe
fuperior fenfe and integrity oppofe prejudice,
and whofe purfuits are confcientioufly regulated by their profeffional motto"—for the
benefit of mankind."

By converfation with feveral of them on
the fubject, I have the fatisfaction from
authority to exprefs their unanimity of fen-
timent: " that a careful revifion of our laws
" is highly expedient, and would fo fimplify
" legal

" legal procefs, as greatly to reduce the ex-
" pence, and render it eafy of accefs to all ;
" though they confefs that fome impediment
" would arife in the branch of conveyancing,
" owing to the various exifting diftinctions
" in the tenure of property." I fee encouragement then, on which to congratulate my country on fome profpect of the accomplifhment of their wifhes ; and am myfelf perfectly perfuaded, that the branch of conveyancing may be as fufceptible of concife modification as any other part of our fyftem of jurifprudence; and that an eftate may be conveyed as fecurely in one as in one hundred fkins of parchment—in ten lines as in ten thoufand ; of which I have lately feen many inftances under a fhort affignment of title-deeds, purpofely devifed and adopted to avoid the enormous expence of a formal conveyance in full legal extent ; *cuftomarily*, and, therefore I fuppofe *neceffarily*, enumerating and recapitulating poffeffors and deeds for a century paft.—

paſt.—Why the poſſeſſion of title-deeds, and a receipt for the money, under a conciſe conveyance, ſhall not ſecure property as effectually, as ſuch recapitulatory deeds now in uſe; —and why an act of the legiſlature ſhould not ſanction a ſummary practice, I ſubmit to the conſideration of the community*.

The extraordinary aſſertions of ſome of the declaratory ſocieties, induced me to en-

---

* Let us advert to a deed of conveyance called an Engliſh POTTAH or title-deed, now in uſe in our ſettlements in India, the depoſit of which, under a form of mortgage, equally conciſe, is implicitly accepted as ſecurity for money. The value of the land is known by its ſituation. The deed is regiſtered, and runs as follows: " A Pottah is hereby " granted unto John Doe, of Lincoln's Inn, for one " hundred acres of land, ſituate, lying, and being in the pa- " riſh of Mimms in the county of Herts, the land-tax of " which is 16l. 6s. 8d. per ann. This land was the property " of Richard Roe, of Gray's Inn, who acknowledges to have " received the full conſideration agreed on for it, and now " relinquiſhes all claim unto the ſaid John Doe and his " heirs for ever."

The whole expence of conveyance and regiſtering does not exceed fifteen pence!!!

ter on this subject, which is treated as a cause of extreme hardship, calling aloud for reform: but from the difficulty of the subject, it is, probably, the least likely to undergo that deliberate and dispassionate discussion, which alone can effect it. To that end, I have however endeavoured to do, what, thus far, has appeared my duty as an individual.

I shall now close this head with recommending to the people of England, to signify their wishes by instructions to their respective representatives in parliament, whose immediate province it is, to explore and revise all the laws, for the purposes of supporting the good, amending those that are bad, and proposing new ones. To enable them to do which, the nation allows a very competent establishment of law-officers. Till that desirable end be accomplished, I shall take the liberty of reminding all my fellow-citizens, whom

whom the formidable chaos of our laws may difcourage, to feek redrefs by another mode, and to refort to friendly and brotherly references of arbitration, in a JURY of Two or THREE, without the formal and expenfive intervention of Courts, Judges, Counfel, and Solicitors, inftead of a JURY of TWELVE which cannot affemble without them. This is a conduct which the great mercantile body of London affociated at Lloyds have moft ftrongly recommended by their example.

SECTION

SECTION VIII.

THE PEOPLE's WEIGHT IN THE GOVERNMENT,
RESPONSIBILITY OF MINISTERS,
AND CONCLUSION.

IN endeavouring to perform what I deem a duty, I shall not apologize to my fellow-citizens for trespassing on their time, in the discussion of the prominent features of the British constitution. I see so many real and solid advantages that I am concerned to think they should not be better understood. It was designed by our ancestors, and it can only be the intention, that every citizen should alike feel and partake of them; and if he does not, I am persuaded that it must proceed from a want of the proper knowledge.

Why should ENGLAND, at this time, be less

less the object of our admiration and affection than at any former period? Not on account of her antiquity; for years have added to her value! It cannot be, that she is no longer willing to administer relief to the poor and helpless, or to employ the young and active in her arts, manufactures, navigation, and commerce! It cannot be that, under a system of protecting laws, her independence is established. Neither can it be, because all these blessings are happily diffused among the people by a gracious Sovereign!!—whose manifold virtues, whether contemplated as a husband, a father, or a friend, both in his public and private character, are undeniable, and whose sole motives are unbounded humanity and affection!

An idea has been industriously circulated, that the people are despised as a multitude and cyphers in the state. The position I should hope to be impossible; and the face of the country stamps it so. A view of the government evidently manifests that, although the established plan of its administration delegates authority to separate estates, in the character of trustees for the community, there can actually be but *one*, and, politically, only *two* parties,—the KING and the PEOPLE; and that there does not exist a middle class. For, what are the nobility but a small number supposed to be selected and dignified by their virtues and services, and politically entrusted, for the BENEFIT of the PEOPLE, with the intermediate situation of a COUNCIL and JURY of the NATION?

The People are the real and solid support of the state; and instead of not existing any where, they are to be seen in all stations, as the prominent figure in the scene. Are they in the management of the government?—
there

there can be no government without them. Are they poffeffed of power? They are,—as being the national truftees conftitutionally appointed by their popularity. Do they make laws for the State? They *wholly* pof-fefs, in their Houfe of Commons, the department which can *dictate* laws. Do they judge of the breaches of thofe laws? We find them in the character of JURORS interpreting and fupporting what they themfelves have enacted as LEGISLATORS. Are their decifions to be fulfilled? We find the people at once obeying and executing; and that without *their* fervices, breaches of the laws would render laws inefficient. Are the people aggrieved? We fee them appealing to *themfelves* in that department of the ftate in which they are purpofely ftationed to defend their liberties, to redrefs their own grievances; and by checking the popular truftees in the abufe of power, and upholding the other two Eftates, as the certain means of

averting

averting oppreffion and difcontents, we behold the people preferving that conftitution which is the bafis of all. Are the people in all the public offices and departments of the ftate? Without them the doors of no affembly would be unlocked. Are they employed in the army and navy? Without them, there could be neither. Do they cultivate the land and employ the manufactures for their own benefit?—Without fuch affiftance the firft would be unproductive, and the latter fall into decay.

POPULARITY v . is another term for the GOOD-WILL of the PEOPLE, is indeed the proud prize of all men:—the *great* ftruggle of ftatefmen:—the only CONSTITUTIONAL method by which they can or ought to become the minifters of the people entrufted with the management of the ftate.

When grievances are felt, the conftitution
which

which tells us, " that the King can do no wrong,"—teaches us alfo, that the caufe is only to be looked for, and can be found but among the PEOPLE:—and in order to afcertain, in what clafs of them, we have but to enquire of OURSELVES, who, among us, has the power to inflict grievances? Or, *who*, being in poffeffion of power, has the opportunity of abufing it?—And, in this enquiry we are, firft, directed to thofe individuals of the people, whofe POPULARITY created them the TRUSTEES of the executive power; and we fhall next advert to fuch part of them as have been felected to fill that department of the ftate, whofe inftitution was defigned as a CONTROUL FOR THE PEOPLE. And, it is here we fhall difcover the fource of the evil.

By thus inveftigating the caufe, we have new reafons to admire the well defigned order of our conftitution; and fhall find our system so perfect, that these departments cannot err separately: they can only do so together and by connivance: for, if the trustees of the executive power abuse their trust, the controuling power, with no less wickedness, must betray theirs. If each perform its controuling functions, neither can be wrong; and no cause of grievance or discontent can possibly exist. For, when they do exist, they can only proceed from such a collusion and combination of the executive and restraining trustees against the people at large, as subverts the fabric of government. It is here therefore, whenever the state becomes disordered, that the people must direct their attention; and, as they wish the constitution to be preserved, must apply the remedy:—to effectuate which, they have the choice of two constitutional alternatives; one of which refers to their representatives; and the other to the crown. They may admonish their respective members individually,

or

or apply to them, in their collective capacity, by petition:—and they can alfo legally, entreat his majefty, to refer the remedy to the people at large, by putting an end to the truft of their reprefentatives by a diffolution of the parliament.

The well known principle of our conftitution, " that the King can do no wrong," can never be too often repeated, or too ferioufly inculcated:—no fyftem of ethics ever contained a ftricter truth: for, our conftitution is fo wifely founded on popular principles, that the king has but the power of doing GOOD. Minifters only are refponfible to the nation at large for every thing that is wrong, be the caufe what it may; their truft and nomination meaning this or nothing. And thus they enter on their duties, under the fevereft penalties to which men can poffibly be fubjected. It is, however, to be lamented, as perhaps the leading caufe of

national

national calamities, that authority once obtained, minifters do not always recollect, either that they are the fervants of the community, or even remember the objects which induced the people to truft them. Some men poffibly confider confiftency of conduct as incompatible with the dignity of general confidence: and few, indeed, are the inftances where the allurement of ftation has been deliberately rejected on a rigid principle of duty. Were the minifters of the people more faithful, or as upright as they muft be when dependant on popular fupport, convulfion would have been lefs known, calamity fcarcely felt, and animofity among nations had long fubfided.

The Britifh government can alone infpire the hiftorian with pride to communicate to pofterity, that amid *fcientific* corruption, when the reprefentatives of nations virtually acted on a fyftem of defection, the people

people of England had the glory to elect **a** minifter, who,—faithful to VIRTUE and HIM-SELF! apprehending a confpiracy among the other truftees againft thofe interefts which the *vox-populi* had ftationed him to defend, and fcorning to become a party, he honourably founded the alarm, and refigned a function that could only prove advantageous to himfelf*. How oppofite to this is the conduct of minifters in general, be their country or the nature of their government what it may. Poffeffed of power, they foon become willing to confider it as committed to them for their

---

* In March 1782, Mr. Fox was chofen Secretary of State. In July following, finding a majority of the cabinet oppofing the expectations of the Nation, he refigned. In April 1783, the voice of the People replaced him. With the lofs of his India Bill, he again quitted his ftation. That Bill would alone immortalize him! Though fupported by the almoft unanimous applaufes of the Houfe of Commons, it was overruled in the Honfe of Lords. It is *now* feen, that the operation of that Bill would have produced *a relief of the burthens of the People to the amount of three millions annually.*

own private advantage, and the support of their partialities and friendships. Their exertions no longer descending to the relief of public burthens, are converted into a system of finance. And merit alone consists in extent of the Excise, assessment, and contribution. Treasure is amassed from the labours and industry of the people. And, the monster thus torn from their bowels and exhibited to view! they are taught to admire and to adopt it, as the happy fruit of ministerial talent.—Ministers have, however, these treasures at their disposal, and use them but as the means of their own support. When we survey a House of Representatives, whose duty it should be to prohibit abuse of power, and waste of money, we see men with views and passions to gratify: and who even go into the assembly in pursuit of places, pensions, and honours. The application of these sources of corruption, supported by extensive armed establishments, frequently constitute the

the whole science of government. And the power to conduct it thus left indefinite, its operation will ever be directed to create finance, in order to multiply patronage, and so perpetuate its own existence.

It is thus that ministers too often become *the sole arbiters of their own conduct*, and like the Decemviri of Rome, hesitate not to unmask and maintain their situations at all hazards. It is thus, that callous to remonstrance, they revile and employ hirelings to decry the conduct of men capable of exposing them as a means of removing opposition. They strive to blind the People against their true friends, and to sow dissention among them, by obloquy, invective, and false imputations. Individuals of them are sometimes seen threatening the cabinet with retiring on their thus acquired popularity, as a means of commanding acquiescence to obnoxious measures: sometimes terrifying the people with

with the force of prerogative. And even under portending conflict to the country, stipulating and contending among themselves for the selection of places or the extent of corrupt influence!

Such practices in any state only warn us to be circumspect in our own, and to feel the happiness of being able to avert them.—Whenever, therefore, attempts are occasionally made to set the King and the People at variance; by inducing the King to doubt the fidelity of the people and the people to be jealous of the royal prerogative, we shall be justified in our construction of the motives of such conduct, in our intermediate agents; and thus trace with certainty the source of our wrongs. Whatever may be the cause of our sufferings, we are directed by the constitution to look for it among ministers, with whom alone our controversies must be. To what else can we attribute all the miseries and

and bloodshed with which England has at any time been afflicted? Our history indeed affords but one instance of any contest really and wholly between the King and the People. I refer to the second James; and here the inequality was so great (which it will always be under similar circumstances) that in order to decide it, the people had but to declare their determination, and to leave the King a free passage by which quietly to effect his escape. The case of Charles the first was different. It was not a contest between the King and the People. It was a struggle between the vicious part of the community, and individuals feeling and acting like men determined on freedom. The former partook of, and, therefore, were attached to a system of tyranny and slavery, concealed under the disguise of divine right, passive obedience, and non-resistance. To these there sprang up a third, and ultimately the prevailing party. This, which had been enabled

to

to erect a standard with the instruments and from the discords of the other two, was, through the ignorance of the People, scandalously suffered to stab the constitution, by pardoning, or rather overlooking those ministers and abettors of the deceived King, whose lives should have been the just forfeit; and inhumanly butchering the Sovereign in defiance of his inviolability. The people at large were doomed unavailingly to repine until the period of the Revolution.

I repeat, therefore, what I should feel myself happy if I could so engrave on the heart of every one, that it should extend itself with time, spurn at all insidious and corrupt attempts to create a jealousy of our beloved sovereign. In every instance of the kind, his exemplary virtues should stigmatize such efforts with the odium of treasonable falsehood. It is only the intermediate trustees of power appointed by ourselves and accountable

accountable to us for their conduct, of whom we have to be jealous; who when we enable them to fulfil their moſt ſolemn pledges for our benefit, ſcornfully forget the hand which foſtered them, and the return due to it; and, thenceforward, only deviſe means beſt calculated to ſtrengthen themſelves under ſuch pretences and ſubterfuges, as the undefined branches of our conſtitution may furniſh to their ingenuity.

Confide, then, in your King, he is the conſtitutional defender of liberty; and the watchful guardian of your happineſs: but, ſuffer not your attention to be aſleep to the conduct of ſuch of your intermediate agents ſtationed as his Miniſters: they alone have the power to injure; and equally poſſeſs the means of deceiving the King, and of impoſing on you. Were theſe agents always as vigilant, faithful and diſintereſted, as you are active in encouraging them by your confidence,

fidence, domeſtic tranquillity would not be liable to violation, or ſurprize; nor could any impudent intrigue, or coarſe, inſulting impoſition be attempted to ſow diſcord; to proſcribe ſome as rebels; and brand all with diſaffection, inſurrection, and ſedition. In a free ſtate, a general ſearch warrant,— incomplete only in legality, is backed by the terrific influence of office, and the hovering menaces of military force,—while the people themſelves indignantly defy the teſt! And at the ſame time prove themſelves good citizens throughout the nation, ſtruggling who ſhall be the firſt to exhibit the pureſt loyalty, the moſt exemplary attachment to the conſtitution, and the moſt rigid ſubordination to legal magiſtrates and to the exiſting laws!

Artifices of the groſſeſt complexion, when ſanctioned by authority, eaſily command the credulity of the people. The extraordinary and

and abrupt manner in which parliament was convened, countenanced the late delufion:— and, judging by events, individuals might be induced to conceive the whole as a pre-concerted plan infidioufly contrived to operate as a cover for fecret purpofes, which, confiftently with the public pledge of neutrality, dared not to be avowed, but which diftant continental connections might eafily lead us to conjecture. It is eafy to deceive,—difficult to undeceive; and this difficulty encreafes in proportion as the original artifice has fpread. But, in this inftance, what expofes the delufion, is a review of the meafures which have been adopted; the fhort fitting of parliament; the failure of an houfe when it had been appointed to meet; the almoft inftant adjournment in the midft of alledged danger; and that too for as long a period as in times of uninterrupted tranquillity;—had there been any real foundation for an apprehended convulfion, the fteps taken were infufficient sufficient to the avowed object. But the adjournment of parliament, has, unequivocally declared to us, that more was not requisite. If the alarm had not been previously suppressed, or the political feint exploded, the removal of which was the avowed object of our national constituents assembling, surely they would never have adjourned themselves. Safety of the state, and duty, had forbidden it. The sitting of parliament always inspires the nation with confidence; it is the stationary *feugal* from whence the people take their motions; and the late sudden call of it was wholly in that spirit. And its early adjournment clearly manifested, that the *storms* of the state were not alarming.

Although the general tremor of apprehension has subsided, the mischievous impression it has left on the public mind is much to be deplored; and it is more than ever

ever incumbent on us to be circumspect in performing our respective duties, by which alone the people can effectually recover their wonted weight and dignity; and the proper balance of government can be restored. It is an evil peculiar to a popular government, that in all extraordinary cases it is liable to be hurried into extremes by the artifices of designing men, who deriving confidence from supposed probity, whenever they depart from that character to suit the necessity of the moment, it is under an artful disguise only that they prevail, and it is so long before the consternation subsides, that the correction of the mischief becomes next to impracticable. Under such an undue influence, a middle way, between licentious opposition and slavish subservience, is difficult. For as the one party acquires, the other proportionably loses strength; and the result generally is such an absolute preponderance on one side, as to be little short of annihilation

nihilation on the other. In such a conjuncture, those who exert themselves to correct a system so destructive in its operation to the order of the state, are the true friends of both, and merit distinguished rewards from their country. Our late agitation evinces this truth. We have seen attachment to the constitution testified at the expence of freedom; and we have seen the censure of a single book, even before its merits had been decided on by the law, considered as a signal for a systematic exertion to annihilate the liberty of the press, that grand luminary, which has already rescued, and which only can preserve the world from ignorance and slavery. By this outrageous attack the rights of mankind have received a wound, to be healed only by the fostering hand of juries, and by an accurate and nice discrimination of their duties and jurisdiction.

BRITONS! We cannot too sacredly venerate

nerate our prefent conftitution, the governing principles of which are in full vigour and luftre, and only vulnerable when we neglect to perform our duty in defending the true balance between liberty and prerogative, as eftablifhed by law. We never can too highly value our now unlimited right of trial and decifion by Jury, which it depends on ourfelves to maintain; and fo long as we preferve it in its purity, it will fupport our liberties, though every other branch of the conftitution fhould perifh. We never can atone, either to the prefent, or to generations yet unborn, for fuffering an injury to be committed againft our juftly-boafted birth-right—the liberty of the prefs. And our unbounded power as jurors, purpofely created for its protection, will render us the more criminal, if we betray that facred truft. We cannot be too watchful over the truftees of power, nor too fcrupuloufly contract their engagements to obtain our confidence,

dence, with their manner of fulfilling their obligations. We never can too seriously resent any unconstitutional interference of a military power, which ought to have no strength but against the enemies of our country.—Nor can we be too tenacious of public freedom, which is but a temporary bequest to be transmitted undiminished to our children. We can never be too confident in a King, who steadfastly rests his throne on the affections of the People; nor too zealously maintain the LIBERTY of BRITAIN;—the protection of which, says Judge Blackstone, " is a duty
" which the People owe to themselves, who
" enjoy it;—to their ancestors, who trans-
" mitted it down; and to their posterity,
" who will claim at their hands, this, the
" best birthright, and noblest inheritance of
" mankind."

F I N I S.

www.ingramcontent.com/pod-product-compliance
Lightning Source LLC
Chambersburg PA
CBHW030408170426
43202CB00010B/1528